ccm *l i f e* L I N E S

Copyright © 1999 by CCM Books, a division of CCM Communications

Published by Harvest House Publishers, Eugene, Oregon 97402

Library of Congress Cataloging-in-Publication Data
Farnsworth, Merrill.
    AVALON / by Merrill Farnsworth
      p.   cm.—(CCM lifelines)
      ISBN 0-7369-0275-9
      1. Avalon (Contemporary Christian musical group)   2. Contemporary Christian musicians—United States
Biography.   I. Title.   II. Series.
ML421.A93F46   1999
782.25—dc21
                                                    99-44487
                                                     CIP

Printed in the United States of America.

99 00 01 02 03 04 / IP / 10 9 8 7 6 5 4 3 2 1

First Edition

Avalon is managed exclusively by Norman Miller and Glenda McNalley, *Proper Management, Nashville, Tenn.*
Avalon is exclusively booked by William Morris Agency, Inc., *Valerie Summers, Nashville, Tenn.*

You can write to Avalon: c/o Sparrow Records, P.O. Box 5010, Brentwood, TN 37024-5010

A publication of CCM Creative Ventures • **Writer:** Merrill Farnsworth • **Art Direction & Design:** Jeff Amstutz
& Michael Miller • **Cover Photograph:** Matthew Barnes • **Interior Photographs:** Matthew Barnes, Tim New

AVALON'S STRIKING LOOKS, "POWER" VOCALS AND HUGE SUCCESS MAKE THE FOUR SINGERS APPEAR untouchable. Michael, Janna, Jody and Cherie may seem more like one-dimensional characters from a fairy tale than living, breathing human beings with complex lives and everyday struggles. But if you could be backstage with them as they pray together before a concert, you would see four people who share the same insecurities and fears as you and me. You would hear

through their prayers a desire to offer up their gifts to God. You

would hear in their voices a genuine concern for those who have

come to hear them sing. You would see in their faces a softness

that reflects, in this quiet moment, God's unconditional love. In

this circle of four, gathered before the One who gave them

voices to sing, you would witness the true heart of Avalon.

ON BEING AVALON

Glitz, fortune, fame, sheer insanity or what?

At first glance Avalon seems pure glitz and glamour; four talented vocalists gifted with charm and good looks. Their teeth are whiter than white, the clothes they wear fit perfectly on their often photographed forms and they are adored by their fans, who flock to

their concerts for a dose of Avalon's trademark high-energy vocal harmonies.

A closer look reveals the hard facts: the grueling touring schedule that keeps them away from home at least two hundred days out of a year, the five o'clock wake up call that comes after going to bed at 2 A.M., the crummy hotel rooms that were booked in the early days of Avalon, waking up at 1 A.M., feeling the bus skid on a patch of ice and wondering if the driver is even awake enough to keep from plunging over the mountainside; waking up with fever and chills and knowing the other members of the group are counting on you to go on stage that night so the band and crew can be paid, having your father die and being on stage three nights later smiling for the fans.

Perhaps the members of Avalon put up with the demands on their lives because the money is fantastic. According to co-manager Glenda McNalley, they could make just as much or more holding down an average 9-5 job. So maybe it's the glamour? Waking up in a different hotel room every morning and getting on a bus to ride all day then sing that night is not exactly living the high life. The fame? Signing autographs and talking to fans after traveling all day, singing for two hours then knowing it's back on the bus and on to the next show doesn't give you much of a chance to revel in being adored by strangers.

Is Avalon just a bunch of young crazy kids out for a good time before growing up and facing normal 9-5 jobs? With all members of the group closer to 30 than 20, the "young kids" part of that equation doesn't hold true. The "crazy" part and the "normal jobs" issue are still up for consideration. However, according to those closest to them, it is God's calling that keeps them relentlessly on the road and in the studio. So for now, Michael Passons, Janna Potter, Jody McBrayer and Cherie Paliotta will answer the call by being a part of the phenomenon known as Avalon.

The following pages tell the story: the creation of Avalon, how the four current members became a part of the group, where they came from, what they are doing now, where they are going, plus fun facts about your favorite Avalon members.

THE
TO A V

1998's NEW ARTIST OF THE YEAR:

Avalon's Michael, Nikki, Janna and Jody proudly accept their first Dove Award.

AVALON

"A Metaphor for Heaven"

— Grant Cunningham,
Sparrow Records A&R Co-creator of Avalon

Avalon smashed onto the Christian music scene in 1996 with their danceable Abba-like vocals, good looks and notoriously hip wardrobe. In 1998, the four vocalists were proclaimed the Gospel Music Association's New Artist of the Year. A year later Avalon captured Dove awards for Pop/Contemporary Song of the Year for "Testify To Love" as well as Inspirational Song of the Year for "Adonai."

With 11 number one hits behind them, Avalon's road seems paved with gold. What makes some acts shine while others struggle to be heard? Talent is one obvious answer and timing another. The four vocalists who make up Avalon are gifted vocalists and the timing was right for their sound. However, another ingredient was stirred into the mix of their instant success—a record contract was waiting for Avalon before Avalon ever existed.

> ...a record contract was waiting
> for Avalon before Avalon ever existed.

WANTED

One Great Vocal Group

This is the age of marketing; find a need, fill it, package it, sell it. Norman Miller is the marketer of note in this tale. Mr. Miller's organization manages such acts as Twila Paris, Margaret Becker, Out of the Grey and Phil Keaggy. It was Miller who packaged and promoted the successful Young Messiah Tour, which played before millions and featured such vocal greats as CeCe Winans, 4HIM, First Call and Sandi Patty.

Miller had the idea to manage a vocal group and took the idea to Sparrow president Peter York. York responded by saying that if the group was great, he was interested.

Thus Miller and York set out to find a great Christian vocal group already fully formed, waiting to be discovered and marketed to record-buying Christians. Their journey took them to places such as Arizona and Pennsylvania, each time hoping the latest undiscovered group was IT. They came up short. Nothing fully formed matched their vision.

The road trips having failed to turn up greatness, it occurred to the two men that the group might be right under their noses. Nashville is always brimming with new talent pouring into town in search of stardom. Nashville's restaurants employ hundred of singers and songwriters who are hoping and praying their big break is one tip away. Despite the great pool of talent, Avalon was not to be found in Nashville's music scene. The search continued...

LET THERE BE AVALON

Enter Grant Cunningham, newly hired A&R genius, fresh from the world of commercial music. For two years, Cunningham had been in the studio working for Hummingbird Productions, writing and singing commercials for products such as Coke, Pepsi, and Wrigley's

Avalon, reaping awards with Grant Cunningham (far left),

the man whose vision brought them together.

Gum. Because he had been working with so many gifted vocalists in the Nashville music community, Cunningham was the natural choice to help create the vocal group Miller and York had been unable to find.

Cunningham put out the word and was immediately flooded with demo tapes. He listened, auditioned and strategized with Sparrow's staff. However, the reality of a vocal group still eluded its would-be creators. It soon became apparent to Grant that the sterile technique of auditioning vocalists, throwing them together in the studio and recording a record lacked soul. He let the vision go for awhile, feeling that if such a group was to form, it must somehow form itself in God's timing.

Cunningham is sensitive to the fact that Avalon has the bum rap of being a "packaged" group. According to him the forming of Avalon was "not that different from the way the guys in 4HIM decided to attach to each other and become something or than the girls in Point of Grace, who happened to form during college. Just because Avalon didn't form in *exactly* the way these groups did doesn't make them any less natural."

The group was eventually named Avalon, which in Cunningham's words, is "a place associated with the legend of King Arthur. It was a place of healing, and the place where Arthur returned after his death. To me, Avalon is a metaphor for heaven, a place of hope for us all—every song Avalon sings ultimately reflects this hope."

[...if such a group was to form, it must somehow form itself in God's timing.]

FIRST CAME MICHAEL

Michael Passons,

"Father Avalon"

Having put Avalon on the back burner, Cunningham went about the business of being an A&R guy, which includes checking out various artists at showcases around town. In February of 1995, he went to hear a songwriter play at a showcase. While he can't recall the name of the singer/songwriter he went to see, Cunningham did remember a guy named Michael Passons, who at the time of the showcase was a successful solo performer.

Michael grew up singing in a small Baptist church in the town of Yazoo City, Mississippi, where his father was a music minister. Michael wasn't aware of the contemporary Christian music scene until he went away to summer camp during his junior-high years. At camp he heard his first contemporary Christian song, "Father's Eyes," by Amy Grant. It was then he caught the vision of a music ministry of his own. By following his desire to sing Christian music, Passons' life intersected with Sparrow's vision of a vocal group that would reach millions.

Grant Cunningham contacted Michael a few days after hearing him perform.

They met at a Cool Springs restaurant, just outside Nashville. Grant explained Sparrow's vision and asked Michael if he would consider being the first member of Avalon. Michael's solo career was going well and he was content to pursue his own music. However, he was intrigued by the offer and agreed to pray about the

> ...it became clear to Michael that being part of Avalon was something he wanted.

opportunity while continuing his solo appearances. After a couple of weeks, it became clear to Michael that being part of Avalon was something he wanted. He called Sparrow to say he was "in."

Today, Avalon's other members teasingly call Michael, "Father Avalon," due to his role as the group's founding first member.

THEN CAME JANNA

Janna Potter,

A Touch of Soul

Although Michael had voiced his willingness to be part of Avalon, Sparrow had made it clear there would be no official contracts signed until the other three members were on board. He went on with his solo career, willing to let the future unfold.

Meanwhile, Janna Potter, a vocalist with Truth, heard of Sparrow's project and was interested in knowing more. She contacted Cunningham by sending a package and a tape. Her letter explained her situation with Truth, and requested that her interest in Avalon be kept confidential. On his way to Estes Park, a gathering of Christian singers and songwriters in Colorado, Cunningham stopped off in Denver to hear Janna perform. Janna was "such a great singer" that he was eager to get her together with Michael as soon as possible. When she had some time off, Janna flew to Nashville to meet the players at Sparrow. Most critical of all was meeting Michael to explore the blending of their voices and personalities.

Janna, a pastor's daughter, had grown up in Baltimore listening to R&B on the radio. She remembers listening to vocalists such as Aretha Franklin and wondering what she could do to "make her voice sound like that." She experimented with her voice, bending it to the tones of black gospel and blues. She discovered a love of

> ...for Janna, those moments when many voices come together as one is a spiritual experience.

singing in groups, playing off the voices of other members. For Janna, those moments when many voices come together and seem as one is a spiritual experience.

Obviously, Janna and Michael's voices came together in a powerful sound that pleased Sparrow. They discovered an instant rapport. Avalon was now a group of two—more than a dream yet not quite a reality.

JODY MAKES THRE

Jody McBrayer,
A Dream Comes True

After two years in California, doing time as a prodigal son, Jody was on the road with Truth. In fact, he and Janna were an "item"—a vocal item. They were known as Truth's "duet king and queen." When Janna quit the group in November of 1995 to join Avalon, Jody was disappointed, but he soon got over any hard feelings, wished her well, and went on with his career.

Janna didn't forget Jody. When she learned Avalon was still in need of "another guy," she immediately thought of Jody and gave him a call. Although Jody was glad Janna called, he dismissed the notion of being chosen for Avalon as crazy. "It will never happen for me," he thought. But the idea grew in him and he couldn't let it go. He remembers the moment, on the road with Truth in St. Charles, Louisiana, that he decided to take the risk of believing his dreams could come true.

A week later he was sneaking up to Nashville to meet with Michael and

Janna. Jody recalls waiting in the lobby of Sparrow's Nashville offices and being overwhelmed while looking at the wall of gold records recorded by the likes of BeBe and CeCe Winans, Steven Curtis Chapman and Carman. The feeling of impossibility once again overtook him. He felt he was a fool to think he could ever be a part of this world.

After a brief wait, Jody was escorted into a room where John Mays, Peter York and Grant Cunningham—all top Sparrow executives—waited to meet him. "My knees were shaking," admits Jody. The meeting went well. Everyone shook hands. He met Michael. He saw Janna. Everyone was very pleasant, but Jody had no idea what anyone in the room was really thinking. Two weeks later came the call from Cunningham asking him to be a part of Avalon. "I must admit," he says, "I hung up the phone and screamed for joy. It was a dream come true."

One more to go.

INTERLUDE

A game of musical chairs

An interesting part of Avalon's lore is that there was one "three" before Jody and two "fours" before Cherie. The first "three" was a singer named Rikk Kittleman who toured with Avalon in 1995 during the Young Messiah Tour. He made the decision to go his own way immediately after the tour was over.

The first "four" was Tabitha Fair, a popular Nashville studio singer who Sparrow's Grant Cunningham had known during his jingle days. She traveled with Avalon for the 1995 Christmas tour, as did Rikk Kittleman, but after he made the decision to leave the group, Tabitha stayed on. Then as the group was readying to record their first project, she was offered solo deals by three different labels. Fair left the group to pursue those opportunities.

Nikki Hassman was the other fourth member until she left the group after signing a seven album contract with Sony via Tommy Mattola, the super-producer who is credited with discovering and developing the phenomenal career of Mariah Carey. Although Nikki signed her deal in December of '97, she continued touring with Avalon through May of '98.

Nikki recorded two albums with the group, *Avalon* and *A Maze of Grace* and was with Avalon when they won a Dove for New Artist of the Year.

Nikki's exit set the stage for Cherie, who recalls being in the audience when Avalon won the Dove for New Artist of the Year. "I knew, at that moment, that I was somehow supposed to be a part of Avalon."

CHERIE THE
ELEVENTH HOUR FOUR

Cherie Paliotta,

Makes it Complete

Cherie was traveling with the gospel group, Soul'd Out, when Tony Morra, Avalon's drummer called. He wanted her to know Avalon was in an intense search to replace Nikki Hassman. Tony encouraged Cherie to contact Sparrow and set up an audition. Cherie found the call unsettling.

Originally from Johnston, Rhode Island, Cherie had recently made the move to Nashville, joined Soul'd Out and called off her wedding to her boyfriend of ten years. It was a confusing time for Cherie. Soon another friend called. It was Mario Sangermano, Avalon's bass player. He also mentioned she should think about seeking the gig as Nikki's replacement. Then a third friend, Dreamworks artist Tina Vail called with the same idea. A pattern was emerging, but Cherie looked the other way.

Having grown up in a warm family with comfortable surroundings, Cherie had become restless with her good fortune. However, moving to Nashville had given her more of challenge than she had bargained for. Although singing with Soul'd Out was fulfilling, the recent breakup with her fiancé had left her feeling "like my heart had been ripped out." She felt she'd given up marriage to follow the Lord's calling on her life and was looking for the next step.

One day in April, Cherie found herself sitting at a table at Nashville's trendy restaurant/club Cafe Milano with Glenda McNalley, Avalon's co-manager. Through her tears Cherie tried to explain that she didn't want to leave Soul'd Out for Avalon, but she had a feeling it was what the Lord wanted. Glenda knew what a great singer Cherie was and had a sense she was the one to replace Nikki. Glenda asked Cherie for a demo tape.

The only tape Cherie had was a country song she'd recorded that day. Glenda popped the tape in her player, listened to two lines of the song and pressed stop. She'd heard enough to know Cherie was *it*. The tape was dropped off at Sparrow's offices a few hours later. Within a week Cherie met Avalon out on the road to test the personal chemistry and the vocal blend. Before she was even sure what had happened, Cherie was the fourth member of Christian music's hottest vocal group.

ONE B

MICHAEL PASSONS

Michael Passons came into the world on October, 29, 1965. Sheltered in the cradle of his Southern family, Michael's first memory is being bounced on his grandfather's knee. Happily, his family was, and is, a close one. Many summers were spent at

camps on the Mississippi coast. On Sunday mornings, the family gathered for worship at the little Baptist church where his father helped lead music. Sunday afternoons were for sitting around the dinner table at his grand-parent's house, enjoying big homecooked meals while listening to family stories. To this day Michael's favorite foods are fried chicken, cream corn and blackeyed peas—preferably cooked by his mother!

Christmas mornings are fond memories for Michael. He recalls the family gathering around a white frosted cake his mother baked, singing happy birthday to baby Jesus. His favorite children's book is Dr. Seuss', *The Grinch Who Stole Christmas*. There is a glimpse of Michael's heart in one of this story's most winsome heroes, Cindy Lou Who, whose innocent faith in goodness and light melted the Grinch's heart and convinced him to give back Christmas.

Michael's musical talent surfaced at age three when he'd climb up on the piano bench and play hymns he'd heard in church. By six he was up in front of the church singing these hymns to the congregation. The "Jesus Movement" of the '70s, which launched the idea of "contemporary Christian music," was just getting started when Michael first showed signs of becoming a professional singer.

Contemporary Christian music was slow in finding its way to Yazoo City. It wasn't until Michael went off to camp in junior high that he heard a recording of Amy Grant's hit "Father's Eyes" and

The Passons family circa 1970—WA, Ruby, big brother Wayne and Michael.

realized there was Christian music beyond hymns and Sunday school songs. He became an avid Amy Grant fan and collected albums and sang her songs.

His own career began to take shape after he graduated from college and joined a group from New Jersey that traveled the country singing Christian music. Eventually, Michael found his way to a solo music ministry, singing in churches all across America. It was not in a church, but at a singer/songwriter's showcase that his life took the turn toward Avalon.

Grant Cunningham, Sparrow Record's A&R man, happened to show up that night to hear another singer. It was Michael, not the singer he'd come to hear, who caught Grant's attention. The next day Michael got an offer to be a part of a new group Sparrow was putting together. This group was Avalon. Three CD's and almost five years later, Michael Passons from Yazoo City is singing hymns before millions.

TIES THAT BIND: Dad, Mom, Wayne and sister-in-law Linda

join Michael at the 1998 post-Dove party.

STORIES FROM THE HEART

Michael tells the story of saying goodbye to his father for the last time.

Y ou never want to get that phone call, but you know someday it will come.

On August 18, 1998, that call came to me. My father was dying.

Rushing home to Mississippi from Nashville gave me the opportunity to think about my father, his life and the life he gave me. Just one month prior to that day, I'd had the chance to spend the whole day with him talking, eating boiled peanuts and drinking Coke Icees. That seemingly ordinary day has become an invaluable treasure.

I got home in time to speak to Dad one last time. "Feed my dogs," he said to me and my brother. Later, as I sat with him he squeezed my hand and blinked,

PROUD PASSONS:

Passons' parents,
Aunt Polly and sister
Janice with their
pride and joy!

trying really hard to communicate. A tear or two rolled down his cheek.

On Sunday morning August 23, he flew away; he went home. Why didn't God just heal his heart? I don't know. But God has been faithful to comfort me and my family. He has provided for my mom and has given us the kind of peace I read about in Phillipians 4:7.

After living through the death of my father, I know God is faithful, even when in the thick of things, it sometimes doesn't feel like it.

A passion for photography...

Born: October 29, 1965 in Yazoo City, MS **Most meaningful verse from scripture:** Luke 1:3-7 NIV **Most significant spiritual experience:** Six days on a wilderness hike in Yellowstone, conversing with God in His beautiful creation, learning about physical endurance and equating it to my spiritual journey **Most meaningful career experience:** Young Messiah Tour 1995 **Most significant role model:** Billy Graham because of his impeccable commitment to living a holy Christ-like life **Most admired historical figure:** Jimmy Carter **Creative interests other than music:** Wildlife photography **Love of my life:** A man's heart is a deep ocean of secrets.

And a Passons for puppies!

52

FAVORITES

Song: "Heart of the Matter" recorded by Don Henley **Movie:** *The Color Purple* **Children's book:** *The Grinch Who Stole Christmas* by Dr. Seuss **Color:** Blue **Place:** My farm in Yazoo City **Actress:** Joan Cusack **Item of clothing:** Old pair of jeans **Daydream:** Being on a beautiful beach on a remote island in the Caribbean **Food:** Mom's fried chicken, cream corn and blackeyed peas **Flavor of ice cream:** Chocolate Chip **Time of day or night:** Dusk **Place to look at the moon:** On that fore-mentioned beach

Fifth grade Christmas musical—
Michael's first lead role

JANNA POTTER

At first glance, Janna is a tall, slender, attractive brunette with a calm, sophisticated, perhaps even cool air about her. But according to those who know her well, Janna's cool demeanor is not aloofness, but a silent strength inherited from her mother.

"My mother embodies everything a woman should be," says Janna. "She is a true Proverbs 31 woman." Janna's mother is her ultimate role model.

Janna, born February 5, 1971, has often been admired for her talent and beauty—and misunderstood for the same reasons. She's learned to take both the positive and the negative with a grain of salt. A pastor's daughter, she is used to living under the scrutiny of those who take it upon themselves to judge her. Her parents taught her that only the opinions of God, family and close friends really matter in the end. In her home, long late night talks with her parents helped shape her character. No subject was off limits. It is obvious that her close and caring family life set the stage for the self-confident woman Janna is today.

Although Janna, the youngest of three children, was born in Florence, South Carolina, she considers home to be Baltimore, Maryland, where her father was a Pentecostal Holiness minister. Growing up, Janna spent hours listening to black gospel and R&B music on the radio. She remembers being deeply moved

Janna joins her
parents backstage
at the Doves

by these powerful voices, and found herself wondering if she could "make her voice" create those same sounds. By this time, Janna, being a member of a musical family, was already performing gospel songs.

Foreshadowings of a singing career came as early as kindergarten when her beloved teacher Gigi Anderson cast her in "I Saw the Donkey." This time of her life was very significant in that she accepted Christ when she was five years old. During that same year, an evangelist prophesied over Janna, saying that one day she would "sing before millions." This prophesy began to unfold when she was asked to join the touring gospel group, Truth. But this was later, after many happy years in Baltimore.

Janna enjoyed a childhood filled with happy memories. Her first Christmas

> [...her elegant figure does not suggest a person who eats everything in sight!]

memory is the holiday she spent with her grandparents eating chicken and dumplings. One other early memory is spending the summer with her aunt and "eating chocolate ice cream." A funny fact about Janna is that she has a tremendous appetite. The reason many people find this humorous is because her elegant figure does not suggest a person who eats everything in sight.

Janna is one of those fortunate people life has treated kindly. She, of course, has ups and downs like the rest of humanity, but it seems God has blessed her with a gentle childhood and a successful career. She remains close to her family, even though they are many miles apart. A new home has also been added to her list of blessings. As a matter of fact, home is her favorite place in the whole world, a place where she can curl up in front of the fire with a Grisham novel and daydream about the Grammy that might one day find a place beside her many Dove awards.

TROPHY GIRL: Janna knew how to graciously accept awards long before her Avalon Dove.

STORIES FROM THE HEART

*Janna Potter remembers the God who never forgets her—
even when things fall apart.*

I am continually amazed at God's faithfulness in my life. There have been many times I have doubted Him, yet He has always come through for me. One of the most trying times of my faith happened two years ago when I experienced a terrible betrayal of love and friendship from people who were close to me. It seemed as if my entire world would fall apart and God was nowhere to be found. I really began to question God as to why He would allow these events to take place. I felt I was carrying out His will (singing and ministering with Avalon) and yet He allowed the worst pain and heartache to consume me.

I eventually began to struggle with depression and anxiety attacks. On the

surface, my life appeared wonderful—a girl who had it all yet I was dying on the inside. My faith began to waver and I wondered whether life would ever be normal again.

Through much prayer and wise counsel, God was able to rebuild my world back together again. As time passed I began to see how He could use difficult circumstances. It makes me stronger yet more dependent on Him.

Janna's cutest little baby face.

Born: February 5, 1971 in Florence, SC **Most significant spiritual experience:** Receiving Christ at age five **Most meaningful scripture verse:** Proverbs 3: 5-6 NIV **Most significant role model:** My mother, who embodies everything a woman should be. **Most exciting career experience:** Young Messiah Tour 1995 **Creative interests other than music:** shopping, cooking, reading, horseback riding **Most admired historical figure:** Princess Diana. I believe she truly loved people. **Love of your life:** My family and close friends

Even without her front teeth Janna was a school days charmer.

62

FAVORITES

Song: "Great Is Thy Faithfulness" **Movie:**
Sleepless in Seattle **Actor:** Julia Roberts and Al
Pacino **Children's book:** *Curious George* **Color:**
Red **Food:** Anything! **Item of clothing:** My platform shoes **Daydream:** Winning a Grammy **Ice
cream flavor:** Rocky Road **Time of the day or
night:** Evening, when I can see the stars. **Place to
look at the moon:** Out in the country

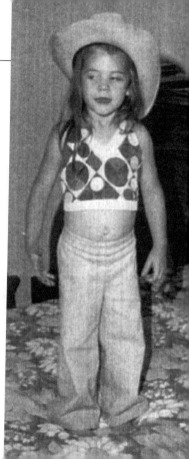

YEE HAW: Janna goes
a little bit country.

TOGETHER ALL DAY: Catching up over morning coffee...

joining Amy Grant
for an impromptu
performance during
an afternoon store
appearance...

and wowing the
audience at an
evening concert.

Avalon keeps on zooming down the freeway of success.

A V A

L   O   N

THE A TEAM:

Avalon with their tour compadrés, Anointed.

GETTING IT RIGHT:

Take after take Avalon perfects their style in the studio.

Friends forever,
Janna and Michael
mug for the camera.

AVALON: Testifying
to Love...live!

WOWIE MAUI: the
gang goes Hawaiian.

I DO: Jody and
Stephanie with
wedding day smiles.

Singing in
the sun.

JODY MCBRAYER

The biggest news in Jody's life is his recent marriage to Stephanie. "I looked into her eyes at the Dove Awards and in that moment, I knew I wanted to spend my life with her," says McBrayer. But to start at the beginning...

The youngest of three brothers, Jody Michael McBrayer was born in Tampa, Florida on June 25, 1970. When Jody was young, his father was the minister at Broadway Baptist Church in Tampa. His childhood was filled with happy memories, "too many for me to pick my favorite." His earliest childhood memory is a trip to Disney World where he was fascinated and charmed by "all the lights in the trees." Summer trips with his parents and brothers to St. Pete Beach were also highlights for Jody.

In his teenage years, Jody attended East Bay High in Gibsonton, Florida, where he joined the school's vocal ensemble group. Jody considered high school a place for having fun. He fondly remembers Mrs. Piddick, his 10th grade English teacher. "She would decorate her room based on whatever book we were reading at the time," he recalls. "She made learning interesting." Even though he enjoyed this particular English class, Jody claims lunch and P.E. as his favorite classes.

Jody takes the cake with brothers Jim and Richard looking on.

When it came time for college, Jody left Florida. He attended Liberty University in Lynchburg, Virginia. He sang in a Christian group, which helped pay his tuition. It was during this time Jody began to feel God leading him toward a career in Christian music. He was roommates with Jason Breland, son of Roger Breland, founder and director of the vocal group Truth. Jason helped Jody get a demo tape together for his father. Upon completing his junior year, Jody left college to join Truth.

After two years traveling the country with Truth, Jody left the group and went to live in California, where his faith was to be tested. Growing up in a Christian home and attending a Christian college had been comfortable for McBrayer. He had never questioned the faith of his parents. But at age 20, he began experiencing great despair and felt unsure of his musical calling.

His father had led him to the Lord when he was 15, now it was time for Jody to make a decision for God apart from his upbringing. Taking on the role of the prodigal son, Jody went out on his own to explore the world. The wonderful world of Disney had always held a certain fascination for Jody, and soon he found himself traveling across the country as one of Disney's featured soloists. He entertained the notion that it was a secular career he wanted more than the life of a Christian artist. But over time, he came to realize that " ... God has an incredible calling on my life and I had to yield to Him." He made the decision to return to Truth as the group's manager.

It was then that Jody got the call from Janna suggesting that he audition for Avalon. Rikk Kittleman had opted to leave the group, leaving an opening for a male vocalist. It was a dream come true for Jody when he got the call from Grant Cunningham welcoming him to Avalon.

Now, with the release of *In a Different Light*, produced by Brown Bannister, there is talk of broadening Avalon's market outside of Christian music. "I get scared sometimes that we are hoarding our own message," says McBrayer, "not allowing it do what it's called to do and that is to go out into all the world. I think we'd be lying if we didn't say that we hope it might have some mainstream success."

As the second half of Jody's life unfolds, perhaps his calling to Christian music will intersect with his former vision of a secular career. In the meantime, he is happy with his life as he knows it.

STORIES FROM THE HEART

Jody McBrayer's tale of life as a prodigal and the loving father who welcomed him home.

There was a time when I believed God was through with me—that He would never use me again for anything. I had messed up royally and disappointed everyone who cared about me. Because of a few bad decisions, I found myself alone, with no one and nothing. I knew in my heart, God did not care either. Or did He? I moved to California and tried, unsuccessfully, to find work in music. Everything I tried for, I lost. These things seemed to push me farther away from anything having to do with the Lord. I became bitter. I was convinced that the Lord was using others more "spiritual" and "flawless" than me. I remember going to church looking for some divine inspiration. I heard all the old clichés that I had heard as a child growing up in church. They didn't help, I was empty. An opportunity finally opened up. I was flown to an audition and felt really good about it when I left. I knew in my heart, "this is it!" I didn't make it. As a matter of fact, I lost horribly and my feelings were hurt worse than ever before. I had to get away. It was time to ask some hard questions to myself and to the Lord. I went away to a hotel on the beach in Southern California. I locked myself in the room for three days and began to pray and read. I didn't even leave to eat. (You *know* I was serious about this!) I remember saying to God, "Lord, I'm tired. Tired of who I am, of what I've become. I want to come home. If all I ever do for You again is take out the trash at church, I'll do it. At least I know I'll be in Your will. I'm tired of pushing for my desires. I want Yours." It was the most pivotal moment of my life. I left that hotel room believing in my heart that I had heard the voice of God. Not two weeks later opportunities began to present themselves and within a month, the Lord had put me back on the road, ministering every night to thousands of people. I never believed God really worked this way until I saw Him actually do it in my life. He truly is faithful.

Born: June 25, 1970 in Tampa, Florida **Most significant spiritual experience:** Obviously, my conversion—when I was 15 my father led me to the Lord. **Most meaningful scripture verse:** Daniel 12:3 NIV **Most significant role model:** My parents. They are the ultimate example of Christ: selfless, caring, loving and always there. **Most exciting career experience:** Winning the Dove in 1998 **Creative interests other than music:** My wife and I are taking hip-hop dance classes. Also reading and traveling. **Love of your life:** My wife, Stephanie

FAST FACTS

Dad and Mom McBrayer proudly pose with their Dove Award winning son (above).

Honeymooners Jody and Stephanie in Maui.

FAVORITES

Song: "You Bring Me Joy" recorded by Anita Baker
Movie: *Sabrina* and *Pretty Woman* **Actor:** Harrison
Ford and Julia Roberts **Children's book:** *Where the
Wild Things Are* **Color:** Silver **Food:** Homemade
cheeseburgers with grilled onions, fresh cut fries and a
big Pepsi **Item of clothing:** My black suit. It goes with
everything. **Daydream:** Living in a house on a cliff
overlooking the ocean in Maui and watching the clouds
roll by as I...daydream. **Ice cream flavor:** Häagen Dazs
Deep Chocolate **Time of the day or night:** Sunset
Place to look at the moon: Maui. Always.

Too young to drive, little Jody gets
some help from his big brothers.

CHERIE PALIOTTA

Cherie Paliotta, the newest member of Avalon, brings the zest of her Italian heritage to the group. She was born in Providence, Rhode Island on May 19, 1970. Cherie lived a sheltered family life, growing up happily with her parents, two sisters and extended family. Fond childhood memories include building a big snowman with "Papa Ralph and Dad and using light bulbs for the snowman's ears," waking up her sisters on Christmas morning and running downstairs to find her first teacup party set and a Barbie, and "finding cookie crumbs that Santa left behind." Her fondest memory is singing "I'm in the Lord's Army" with her little sister Cathy in the camper while on a family trip.

During her high school years, Cherie was an enthusiastic member of the majorette squad. A significant event of her teenage life was meeting a boy with whom she was to have a ten-year dating relationship. They dated through college, where she graduated with a degree in education. She landed a fulfilling teaching job, lived at home and continued her long-term romantic relationship with her boyfriend. Her life was comfortable. "Too comfortable," states Cherie. As perfect as everything seemed, she felt restless.

A friend of hers, who was the director of a group named Soul'd Out, had called her several times, asking her to consider leaving teaching to join the group. She finally agreed and made the move to Nashville. Six months after moving, Cherie's boyfriend proposed. Life was busy traveling with Soul'd Out and planning her dream wedding.

SISTERLY LOVE: Cherie with her siblings Lori and Cathy.

Then three months before the long-awaited ceremony, the wedding was called off.

"It's been a struggle," says Paliotta. "I felt like I had to choose between my boyfriend of ten years and this thing God called me to do. I had been praying and fasting and asking the Lord to show me His will. I had gone to church and was praying at the altar when a man came up and told me, 'The Lord wants me to tell you to stand firm in your decision. I don't know what that means, but He wants me to tell you to stand firm in your decision.'"

Cherie goes on to explain that calling off the wedding was the most difficult decision of her life. She felt as if her heart had been ripped out. A battle with deep depression cast a dark shadow on her life. "I told myself everyday to rest in the fact that God is preparing the right person for me. If my boyfriend of ten years had been the right person, it would have worked out." Ironically, on the day that was supposed to have been her first year wedding anniversary, Cherie found out her former fiancé had already made plans to marry someone else!

Cherie is on an emotional high these days. She just celebrated one year with Avalon and is making plans to settle down in Nashville. Having braved leaving the comforts of her Rhode Island home, Cherie has found a new family in Avalon and is putting down roots in Nashville. And, of course, back in Rhode Island, her parents and sisters are following her adventures and cheering her on every step of the way.

STORIES FROM THE HEART

Cherie Paliotta learns lessons the hard way—and tells the story of God's amazing grace.

God has been doing so many things in my life since I moved to Nashville, but the biggest lesson I've been learning is how to trust in Jesus at all times and not just when things are good. When Jesus seems so far away, that is when we are to trust in His power over our lives even more. This is a difficult one for me. It seems like the longer I take to learn this one, the more trials I have to overcome. I heard a preacher say once, "God is a loving father and when we don't learn the lesson the first time, He will gently teach us the lesson again." What always amazes me is that I've always believed in His power for other people. I could convince you that He can heal you of any sickness, free you from financial bondage, restore broken relationships and the list goes on. Of course, these are all things with visible results. Unfortunately, God's power in emotional healing is the one area I struggle with. We can't necessarily examine these things with a stethoscope or take some kind of medicine to cure it. I've experienced this before; emotional pain that feels like someone has ripped your heart out of your chest and crushed it into a thousand pieces. I must have cried a sea of tears and washed away a world of dreams in the process, yet somehow, the well never runs dry. It's been three years since I experienced my own personal trauma and one would think that by now, the pain would be gone and all the pieces of my broken heart would be mended. But somehow, more pieces keep showing up. Then I have one of my father/daughter discussions with God and ask Him "What's the holdup, Dad? I thought you healed me of this thing last year. We kicked this thing together—I wasn't going to cry about it anymore. You've worked out all of the other areas of my life so why are You waiting on this one?" Of course, this conversation between God and me will go on for days and then suddenly, He finally gets through my thick Italian skull. The answer is simple, it's all according to His time schedule. Every single dream and desire He has for us, He's working it out according to His will in relation to the exact moment that He sees fit. In the meantime, we have to learn to be obedient in the process and trust that He has every good intention. There are many days where I'm struggling with His timetable, and it's difficult to get up on that platform and say, "God is so faithful." But I know that God has called me to be a witness and I have to speak the truth even if it's only in faith at that moment. I know God will bless me because of my obedience. I think that people's perception of our group is that everything is always peachy perfect in Avalon land, but that is not always the case. We are human and we have areas of struggle just like everyone else. Right now, God is teaching me the very lesson I need to learn: Emotional wounds may be different than physical wounds but the Bible says there is nothing too big for my God.

FAST FACTS

"So, let me tell you how it all started..."

Born: May 19, 1970 in Providence, Rhode Island

Most significant spiritual experience: A prophet named Michael Ratlif prophesied over my life one year before Avalon. He said things that only I know and spoke of the future. It all bore such witness to my heart. **Most meaningful scripture verse:** Psalm 116:15 NIV **Most significant role model:** My parents. Despite many obstacles in their lives they bent over backwards to make my life seem like Disney World. They always put God first and gave much love to us.

Most exciting career experience: Singing with CeCe Winans and Crystal Lewis **Creative interests other than music:** Drama class, journalism, creative writing, art: oil and acrylic painting as well as three-dimensional design

Love of your life: Singing, the Lord and my parents

Dad and Mom, Ron and Cheryl Paliotta.

FAVORITES

Song: "Because You Loved Me" **Movie:** *Pretty
Woman*...because it displays how love can repair a
broken life. **Actor:** Julia Roberts **Children's book:**
Where the Wild Things Are **Color:** Blue **Food:**
Chicken Parmigiana **Item of clothing:** Gap boot
cut jeans **Daydream:** Getting married and having
twins **Ice cream flavor:** Rocky Road **Time of the
day or night:** 5-6 P.M....because I love sunsets!
Place to look at the moon: From an airplane

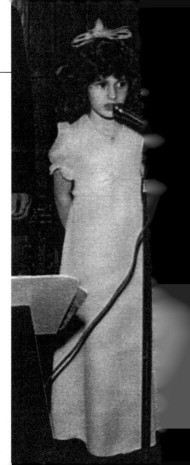

"JESUS LOVES ME THIS I KNOW"

Cherie's musical debut

LAUGH

THE

SWEET DREAMS

Twila Paris is known for giving gifts of very fine chocolate. On Valentine's Day, while touring with Avalon, Twila bestowed her thoughtfulness on the members of the group. They were in Manhattan, and that night, while Avalon was off the bus, Twila secretly placed lovely wrapped chocolates on each of their pillows.

Michael and Jody were so wiped out by that night's concert, and the cumulative effects of touring, that they dove into their bunks without ever turning on the lights. Jody awoke the next morning to the sight of Michael smeared with chocolate. Michael stared back at Jody with a quizzical look on his face, wondering why Jody, who had chocolate smeared all over his face and in his hair, was laughing at him.

TOUR MATES:
Twila Paris (center)
and father/son duo
Aaron + Jeffrey made
sweet music on the
road with Avalon.

When Twila heard of the gift gone awry, she felt awful (after she managed to stop laughing). As it turns out, the guys weren't at all miffed about waking up with chocolate smeared all over them, they were just upset about missing out on savoring the rare and delicious treat.

SOLID GOLD

It was the last concert of the 80-city "Gold" tour. Avalon had been traveling the country with Crystal Lewis, her husband and two small children. "It's like we became surrogate parents for Isabella and Solomon," says Michael. "Crystal and Bryan welcomed us into their lives as part of their family."

But now the tour was ending; Avalon would return to Nashville, Crystal and her family to Los Angeles. However the atmosphere was anything but gloomy that night. "We were all feeling punchy from the months on the road," recalls Passons. Everyone knew a lasting bond had been formed and that this final concert would not be goodbye.

High spirits reigned as the bus pulled into the church that afternoon. As Avalon walked through the church, they discovered a closet filled with every costume imaginable. It was obvious this congregation was into drama. The group had fun looking through the wigs, shoes and glittering clothes. Soon it was time to move on to the sound check.

That night Avalon opened the concert with their high-powered song "Knocking on Heaven's Door." The audience was dead. There was not a smiling face in the house. Not one foot tapped. No one moved. Avalon picked up the pace and gave the song their all. They hit the final notes of the song and waited for the customary applause. Not a sound.

Suddenly Crystal appeared on stage and informed the audience they could now applaud and the crowd went wild. As it turned out, Crystal had arranged to have several "helpers" stand at the doors as the crowd entered and tell them to sit stoned-faced until she appeared on stage. Crystal was quite proud of her practical joke.

When their set was over and they walked off stage, Avalon was of one mind— "TO THE COSTUME CLOSET!" Janna and Cherie dressed in the flashiest costumes they could find. They donned blond wigs and walked the Crystal walk.

DISCO DAZED: Crystal Lewis with her Night Fever dancers.

Michael found an Afro wig and Jody completed the foursome in classic disco style. After a quick rehearsal Avalon waited backstage for a signature Crystal Lewis up-tempo number, then exploded onto the stage unannounced.

It was disco time. Crystal didn't miss a beat as Avalon broke into their own brand of Saturday Night Fever. The audience danced along, hooting and hollering with glee as Crystal hit the final note and Avalon managed to strike a spontaneous disco pose. It was a fun and glorious finale to a tour filled with lots of laughter.

LEFT BEHIND

Avalon was in Oregon. It was Cherie's first time out with the group and she was was feeling some nagging doubts about whether or not she really belonged with Avalon. Michael, Janna and Jody were so close to each other, and Cherie wasn't quite sure if she would ever fit into the "family."

Early that morning, the bus pulled into a truck stop where there was a McDonald's. Everyone who got off the bus was supposed to put their laminate name tag on the bus driver's seat so he would know who had gotten off the bus. He knew not to leave until everyone had collected their name tags and his seat was empty. When he saw all was in order, the driver pulled out of the truck stop and onto the highway.

Meanwhile, Cherie was inside on the phone. She hung up and went out to get on the bus. One problem—there was no bus. True to her Italian nature, Cherie very emotionally searched for the bus, then placed a very emotional call to Glenda, her manager. It was 7 A.M., the bus had left her, she had no money and she was all alone! Glenda calmed her down, called a band member's cell phone and asked if they realized they were speeding south without Cherie. No. They didn't.

Cherie was in tears, wondering if

she had made the mistake of her life by joining Avalon. Glenda once again calmed her down and placed a call, this time to the crew bus. The plan was for the crew bus, traveling an hour behind the other bus, to rescue Cherie. There was a glitch. The crew bus had taken a route which put them on the other side of the mountains. The valiant crew, however took a winding road back over the mountains, several hours out of their way to rescue Cherie. As they were getting off the exit toward the truck stop, the crew bus broke down. A few of the crew members, having heard from Glenda how distraught Cherie had become, hiked to the truck stop to inform Cherie that help was on the way.

To this day, it is not clear what happened to Cherie's nametag. However, Glenda, the faithful manager, is philosophical about the event. "It gave Cherie a story to tell," she says. "That's what being part of a family is all about, right?"

ETCE

BRAZIL '99!

What Avalon did on their summer vacation

n late June of 1999, Avalon traveled to Rio de Janerio with *Brio* Magazine. *Brio* is Focus on the Family's answer to *Seventeen* magazine. The publication offered its readership the opportunity to join a mission trip to Brazil. Four hundred girls responded, saying they wanted to make the journey. Avalon was asked to join the group. The girls and Avalon packed their bags and made their way to South America. While in Rio, they stayed in military housing. All of the girls participated in a drama ministry organized by the sponsors.

Janna, Cherie, Jody and Michael were touched by the lives of the girls who opted for a mission trip to Rio instead of the usual summer activities of camp or the beach, and were impressed with how enthusiastically the girls reached out to the children. They hugged strangers without hesitation, communicated love without knowing Portuguese and ministered tirelessly through drama, song and the simple giving of themselves. Michael remembers a girl who was praying for the children in an orphanage. "Her tears were so heavy with compassion that you could see puffs of dust appear when her tears hit the dirt. They were the most real tears I have ever seen."

The trip made a huge impact on Avalon. "Even the bad parts were good," said Michael. He went on to explain that during their stay they were exposed daily to conditions of extreme, humiliating poverty. "It was difficult to witness the suffering of these people. It was obvious they were good people who wanted to work and care for their families. Now I know better how to pray for these people and realize that I need to do more than pray. I need to offer my resources."

Michael spoke of a community called Lixao, which means "the great dump." A trash dump is literally where the men, women and children in Lixao live. Trash is piled high against the flimsy cardboard structures the residents call home. "The smell was overwhelming," reports Michael, who claims to have a strong stomach. "I didn't want to offend these people by letting on how bad it smelled," he said. "At first it took all my willpower to focus on the people and not the surroundings." But soon he and the other members of Avalon were able to focus in on what really mattered.

There was a man with an infected foot who lived in one of the filthy cardboard structures. Michael entered his house and prayed for his health. The man was very touched by his caring. Michael's voice is soft as he recounts what became a sacred moment. "On the way out of his home, I bent over to get though the door and some of the dirt from the walls got on my hat." Michael explained that for him, the dirt became a symbol of leaving comfort and entering a place of need, "even if it means getting dirty."

The trip to Brazil was not without its dangers. They ministered in one community where not even the local police dared to go. This place, an example of

MISSION POSSIBLE: Michael and neighborhood children from the slums

of Rio watch a drama performed by the *Brio* girls.

unbelievable substandard living, was ruled by a group of men known as "the bosses." Their translator, an American woman raised in Rio, went to the bosses and asked permission for the group to go into the community park and perform a drama. After some discussion, the bosses warily agreed to her request.

The girls, Avalon and others from the *Brio* team went from door to door, letting the residents know of the event. The frightened people huddled in their shabby homes, until a member of the household came forward to ask the question that could be a matter of life and death—"did the bosses give permission for you to be here and for us to go from our houses?" Fortunately, the answer was "yes."

Soon a big crowd gathered in the run-down park. The Brazilians stared at these well-dressed strangers who had sought and received permission to enter their dangerous neighborhood. The peoples' hearts were deeply touched by the American girls who had come all this way to a place most people avoided like the plague.

A festival-like atmosphere descended on the little park. There was music, drama, dancing, laughter and singing. This time of happiness was an oasis for those weary with wondering where the next meal would come from. And then, like a miracle, women and children appeared with bottles of soft drinks made with a cherry-like fruit grown along the Amazon and freshly baked bread. Like the loaves and the fishes, the food was passed around, and somehow, in spite of the unspeakable poverty surrounding them, they all enjoyed a feast to be remembered.

Perhaps this trip marks a beginning for the members of Avalon to have an impact on the world, or perhaps this is an experience that will simply fade over time as they go about the business of their lives. However, whatever transpires in the hearts of Avalon, there are hearts in Brazil who will remember the day "the bosses" allowed the Americans into their park to sing, dance, feast and share the love of the One who had brought them all together.

TAKING CARE OF BUSINESS

How managers manage to manage!

I f an artist is lucky, they have a manager who is honest and does not fall prey to the temptation of taking advantage of them financially or emotionally. If they are blessed, they have a manager who genuinely cares about them. In this area, Avalon is richly blessed to have both Glenda McNalley and Norman Miller as their managers and their friends.

Not only does Avalon's management book flights, procure the best hotel rooms possible, schedule photo shoots, insist they play the best venues, schedule their extensive tours, make sure they show up for meetings, and make themselves available to Avalon by phone or fax 24 hours a day—managers also orchestrate the larger career decisions every artist must make.

Avalon together with the ones who keep it all together! Glenda McNalley (far right) and video director Eric Welsh (center) join Avalon at the "In Not Of" video shot.

And while looking out for their best interests, managers also get to see the warm and wonderful aspects of their artists' personalities that others might miss—just like a friends!

"Take Janna for instance," Glenda says. "Janna is one of the kindest, most genuine and classiest women I know. She is very calm and she never lets her emotions run out of control. Some people take her quiet strength as aloofness." Asked if Janna is ever troubled by being misunderstood, Glenda laughs and comments that Janna is one of the most well-balanced and confident people she knows. "Such a woman never lets the opinions of strangers get her down."

While being quizzed on Avalon's rap of being merely a marketer's vehicle to sell records, her eyes flash. She personally resents the four vocalists being reduced to a merchandising ploy. When asked if there is truth behind the gossip that there is little substance behind the hip clothes and the attractive facades, Glenda responds firmly, "Sure they look good and sound great—that's what the fans want! These are four real, genuine people who have hearts for God."

Preach on, Glenda!

KEEP YOUR EYES ON AVALON AS THEY CONTINUE TO MAKE THEIR MARK IN THE NEW MILLENNIUM. Their CD *In A Different Light*, produced by legendary producer Brown Bannister, is turning out several number one singles. There is a buzz they will soon be following in the footsteps of Amy Grant and Michael W. Smith by extending their music to the secular pop market. Their extensive Fall '99 tour will put them before thousands of new fans.

When asked about their smashing success and the road that lies ahead of them, the members of Avalon speak in one voice, "As we journey through God's perfect will, we can't always see what lies ahead, but we can hold onto the promise that He holds the treasures for those who obey His call."

DISCOGRAPHY
1999 In A Different Light
1997 A Maze Of Grace
1996 Avalon

#1 SINGLES
"Can't Live A Day" #1 AC
"Take You At Your
  Word" #1 AC
"In Not Of" #1 AC
"Reason Enough" #1 AC
"Knockin' On Heaven's
  Door" #1 AC
"Adonai" #1 AC/INSP
"Testify To Love" #1 AC*
"Give It Up" #1 AC
"The Greatest Story" #1 AC
"This Love" #1 AC
"Picture Perfect World"
  #1 INSP

* "Testify To Love" made history
when it remained the number one
song for six consecutive weeks—
making it the longest-running Adult
Contemporary song in the history
of the CCM Update AC chart

AWARDS
1999 Dove Award Pop
  Contemporary Song
  of the Year—"Testify
  To Love"

1999 Dove Award
  Inspirational Recorded
  Song of the Year—"Adonai"

1999 Dove Award Long
  Form Video of the Year—
  "My Utmost For
  His Highest"

1998 Dove Award—
  New Artist of the Year

1998 Dove Award—
  Special Event Album
  of the Year (for their
  contribution to God
  With Us)

1998 CRR (Christian
  Research Report)—
  Group of the Year

1998 CRR (Christian Research Report)—#1 AC Song of the Year "Testify To Love"

1998 American Songwriter Professional Songwriter Award—Artist of the Year

1998 American Songwriter Professional Songwriter Award—Song of the Year "Testify To Love"

TELEVISION APPEARANCES

CNN Headline News
Good Morning Texas (ABC)
AM Nashville (NBC)
Good Day Atlanta (FOX)
A.M. Northwest (ABC)
Good Day Dallas (FOX)
Good Day Kansas (ABC)
Talk of the Town (CBS)
Home Life TV (*syndicated*)
CeCe's Place (Odyssey)
The 700 Club (Family Channel)
100 Huntley Street (Canadian)
Hour Of Power (*syndicated*)
Life Today (*syndicated*)
Donnie McClurkin Christmas Special (BET)

TOURING

1995 "The Young Messiah Farewell" Tour
1995 "Emmanuel" Tour
1996 "Where I Stand" Tour with Twila Paris
1997 "Young Messiah" Tour
1997 "My Utmost For His Highest" Tour
1998 "Gold" Tour with Crystal Lewis
1998 "Christmas Celebration" Tour
1999 "A" Tour with Anointed

For daily updates on Avalon,

visit their web site at www.avalonlive.com